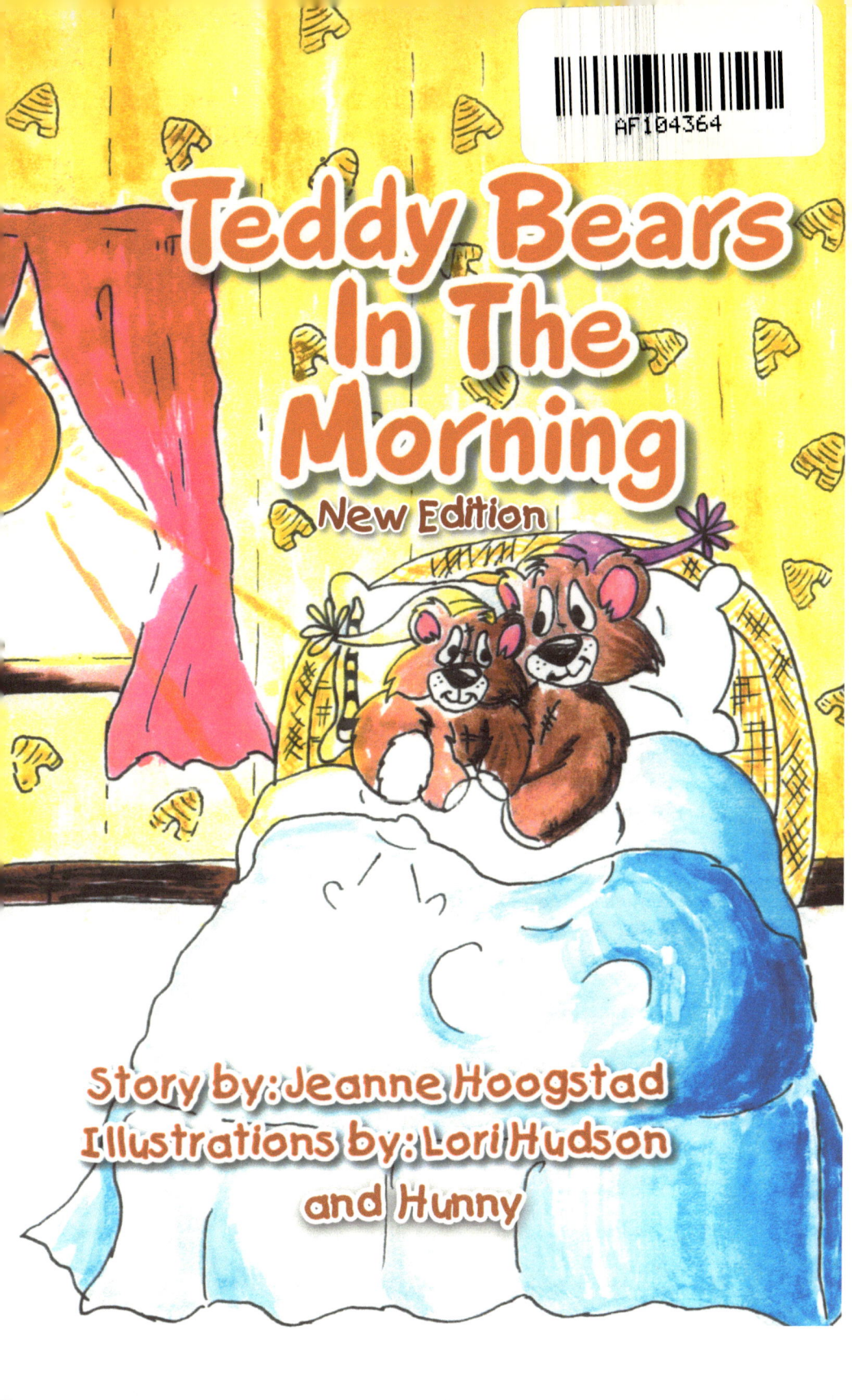

Copyright © 2024 by Jeanne Hoogstad

ISBN: 978-1-77883-322-9 (Paperback)

978-1-77883-323-6 (E-book)

All rights reserved. No part of this publication may be reproduced, distributed, or transmitted in any form or by any means, including photocopying, recording, or other electronic or mechanical methods, without the prior written permission of the publisher, except in the case brief quotations embodied in critical reviews and other noncommercial uses permitted by copyright law.

The views expressed in this book are solely those of the author and do not necessarily reflect the views of the publisher, and the publisher hereby disclaims any responsibility for them.

BookSide Press
877-741-8091
www.booksidepress.com
orders@booksidepress.com

Story by: Jeanne Hoogstad
Illustrations by: Lori Hudson and Hunny

Up from Bed

Through the doorway,

Down the hall,

To Mom's room.
Not here!

Through the doorway,

To the living room.
Not here!

Through the doorway,

Down the hall,

To the bathroom.
Not here!

Through the doorway,

Down the hall,

To the basement.
Not here!

Through the doorway,

Down the hall,

To the laundry room.
Not here!

"Her purse and keys are here,"

"Through the doorway, down the hall"

# Here's our Mother!

www.ingramcontent.com/pod-product-compliance
Lightning Source LLC
LaVergne TN
LVHW070047070526
838200LV00028B/412